Marsha's Well
and
Other Poems

L. C. Fothe

This book of poetry is dedicated
to my loving wife, Marsha
who made every word possible.

Table of Contents

Azure Eyes

Buttery soft – it was the way the air rolled by
Gardens of the mind in bloom all year round
Many are the miles travelled under orchid skies
Knotted packets cradling precious dreams inside;

Across vast spaces where wishes become needs
Blackness flees under the brilliance of visions
In which flying free within rays of sun triumphs
While elation becomes the constant companion;

Clear are the Azure eyes high above the tempest
Arms free to embrace the delicate clouds like lilies
Crisp reflections bounce on projection screen whiteness
Others join in the exuberance of this slow rolling flight;

Where shall we go – to the stars within the heavens?
Let us disappear into the vast realms of creation
Scattering ourselves in tiny specks of brilliance
Shedding light and hope to eyes for eons to come.

Good Morning to Me

I look at my coffee cup, wondering if I should have
    some more,
Is it time to wake up or time for more sleep?
A bird is chirping though the sun is not yet rising
It feels like the companionship I need.
    Dreams I cannot remember have been left behind
    Even though they were so important at the time
    How is it we can be present and fully participating
    Yet have no recall of the arduous events?
Another glance at my empty cup must mean I should
    have more,
The aroma of fresh brewed still hangs in the air
I believe the bird outside is cheering me on
Funny how any excuse seems like the right one.
    Too many thoughts of what needs to be done
    Flood my mind because they all demand money
    It seems so early in the morning to withstand
    Where disappeared the oblivion of sleep?
The cup is now in my hand, finger through the loop,
The sun is rising in its golden glory
The bird song is joined by many other voices
The coffee steaming in my cup tastes oh so good
    this morning.

Relentless

My words have been taken away

Forced into necessary retirement

I saw them fly away in the form of a dove

I know I will never see again

Concrete may buckle, planets may collide

A piece of myself turned to dust in the night

Fences with gates flung wide

Galloping disappeared into careless wind

The "we" was always just me

Thinking I could meld into another

The pot of gold though has reverted to lead

Thought is now thick like tar on a post

I try to fight my way through seething anger

Wishing to find beauty ahead of immense sadness

The words of expression fail to materialize

As sorrow for myself takes center stage

Relentless

I wish the dove would have taken me instead.

If Only

Repetitive visions bring repetitive thoughts of desire
For wishing to have the freedom of a running squirrel
Or the soaring flight of a majestic red-winged blackbird
Through whom I could build a fantasy empire.

Could I learn to run right on all four strong limbs
Using two to daintily manipulate and open seed?
Could I cope with two feet to take the place of hands
With wings for balance and graceful higher flight?

What contrasting differences to wish to aspire!
Both being statements of their own types of freedom
I know neither inherently possesses such altruistic reality
Yet my dreams are scripted by my own magnifier.

I could imagine life being lived in a self-built nest
In branches away from predators but near the sun
Then perfectly dry days of successful foraging
With quiet sleeping nights with a mate closely pressed.

A living of natural life, signals to chitter or to sing,
Going and coming through only the meaningful passages,
Breeding, nurturing, raising another same generation
Sleeping without anxiety as to what a normal tomorrow
      will bring.

On the furry tail or the long feathered one
I would wish to ride as either one of them
If it were possible for me to be accepted
As myself seeking a refreshing brand of welcome.

Windowless Room

Passageways become cluttered

Lost memories litter the floor

I trip over crumpled plans

The ability to see forward is myopic;

Miracles float free elsewhere

My head is a gyroscope

Legs too weak to walk away

Thunder calls to me

Fresh brewed cafés

Slip across the horizon

Ropes to climb high

Crumble into powdery ash

I cannot see beyond my feet

I cannot feel beyond my heart

Nothing I touch can come to me

Words in the wind find no echo

Close my eyes in prayer

Believe beyond my comprehension

Look within for a lost kingdom

Even my tears fall abandoned

Closer Than Close

Softest whispers held such power
    Glowing as climbing inner light
Her eyes were wide like origami unfolding
    His mind filled with cherry blossom scent.

Hand-in-hand they would talk
    The world a backdrop of love
Closeness spoke words of its own
    Binding secrets of intimate being.

Protection they gave to each other
    Intimacy being an impenetrable shield
Humanness making them greater than themselves
    Silver stars against universal black their symbol.

"Where shall we take ourselves today?"
    She gazed into the quiet of thought
His imagination spoke the excitements
    Her smile gave the mark of accession.

Safe in their inseparable natures
    Floating in a frame of foreverness
Keeping their shared secrets hidden
    Changeless smiles remained on their lips.

Across a Welcome Meadow

He sat in quiet contemplation
Hint of a smile on his face
Her image crossed the meadow
In memory of summers' past
When warm breezes brushed their cheeks
Lips touched in gentle heat
Promises held gifts of permanence
Futures called forth their adventures.

Together, sitting at stream's edge,
Laughing in embraces of freedom
Feeling the clear flow of life
Watching glistening sunshine winking
On surfaces of exciting mystery
Recalling memories of the womb
Speaking hopes, wishes, dreams
Sharing thoughts of what could be achieved.

She had picked flowers of the meadow
Purple, yellow, white clusters beckoning,
Held them close like newborn infants,
Savored the aromas of blossomed beauty,
Brought her prizes to thirsting vases

Displayed on desirous window ledges,
Together they marveled at intricate
      designs
Delicate petals to match their vows.

Years all lived there in his mind
Heart filled with the greatest love
No regrets or remorse to surface
Only abounding spiritual oneness
His arms wrapped around her always
Eyes reading their inner secrets
Together forever in the breezes of summer
Quiet contemplation filled his days.

What Will Be Found

A mountain called and I ran
Right up to the rock-face to climb
Knowing I was no mountaineer
I sought passageways for my ascent
Hoping I could somehow find God
Or Jesus or one of the prophets
There amongst the silent stones
In brush and wild bushes
Waiting to show fire without burning
And brightest white lights of purity and
Holiness.
I want my prayer to be like that of Jesus
Where I can physically withdraw from the world
Concentrate fully on a union with God
The spirit within me enlivened by His presence.
May the mountain be imaginary
Without physical form
Just as the Spirit of God
Let the intent suffice that I may find
That for which I seek
Though I may not feel worthy in my own heart
I trust God finds worthiness in me as His child.

Home

Sometimes I wish I could go home
Even when I don't really know what that means,
It is not the house in which I was raised,
It is not the place in which I now live
Though both were known as home
These are not what my yearning is calling for.
Home is a gut reaction to where I feel I belong
It is full safety, nurturing, loving and effortless
For me, it is a natural state of being
Where the fullness of being me can be expressed,
Where I feel the worthiness of being loved
Where my love for others requires no question
I want my home to be where there can be no doubt,
The place of unquestionable permanence in beauty,
Days and nights in which nothing hides,
Where waking and sleeping dreams meld into one,
With me comprehending the purpose of all things.
Yes! Listen to the longing plea in my voice,
Hear the tone of honesty and devotion,
Learn the full meaning with me when I say,
"I want to go home."

Liquid Peace

I was passing through speckled sunshine

As I searched for invigorating rain

To wash me clean by bringing liquid peace

When ten ducks in a "V" glided overhead

Calling like a drill team on a pond-based mission;

I wandered through meadows and fields

Alive with honey bees, butterflies, and foraging squirrels

In my obsession with my quest.

I stopped to watch the grazing of horses and cattle

In pastures of finely presented deep green ;

I could sense a long gone dog scampering before me,

Inviting me to games of running and

    chasing just for fun;

In tall grass is where I chose to sit

Waiting for the special one to come

From whom I could hear the voice for which I longed,

To breathe in the scent of true love and safety,

To feel once again the promised beauty of the world;

The tallness of the surrounding green hid my face

With its silly smile of wished for anticipation –

Eyes with inner light of remembered times in the sun –

The warmth of another hand to hold other than my own;

There were times in my life when 'alone' was just a word –

A state of no one else being there at the moment,

Now, instead, settled the visceral reality from loss –

The one horror I tried so hard to run away from,

Where I listen for the familiar and wait for the sound

Of my name being called, knowing together is only an
    instant away;

In the distance came the rumble of thunder while

The speckled sunshine began to fade

So I moved under a sprawling oak tree

To sit amidst the strong roots and fallen leaves;

Heavy drops began to fall in a gentle chaos of
    beginnings,

Smiles sank from my face along with joyful memories

My hands came to my cheeks and came away

With more than just simple raindrops;

No more tall grass to hide my pain

No more hiding in the center of nowhere

Yet a spark within my chest

Was willing to secretly wait

For the sound of my loved one's voice

Coming across a green meadow.

Songs of Life

It was all inside of the mind

When the stage appeared beneath my feet

I knew they were watching,

The notes flowed from my mouth in flowers

I don't care if you didn't understand

Why I would want to sing those songs;

I could only use my vocal talents

To make you feel things you couldn't on your own.

So many things make me write what I do

The words are statements of who I am,

Even those of who I wish to be,

They are my hand stretching into the darkness

To feel I am not alone

Struggles are useless without their rewards,

Heartaches are futile without the victory of love

My songs express reasons for the train we're on –

The destinations in store up ahead,

The necessary dropping points of unrepeatable pasts

For the joy of forward anticipation of the future to be felt.

I will continue to sing loudly from this stage

My mind will fill in the lights and the crowd

I will sing all of what I know to be true

Because of my love for you.

Open Arms

The woods can hold such secret paths
Letting feet fall upon the history of leaves
Simultaneous freedoms of being on display
Dances with God celebrating in the breeze
Curious innocent birds watch from perches
High within branches of protective trees
Chipmunks make their chattering sounds
As they warily eye strange passersby;
If there is such a thing as quiet in a joyful way
The woods exude the sound in dramatic fashion
Sprouts and buds and proud puffed mushrooms
Feasts of blossoming life bringing tears to the eye
Songs of cardinals and bluebirds provide auditory bliss
Discovery in the aromas of a refreshing dampness
Beneath a subtle canopy of calm uniqueness
A lizard bounds up the lumpy bark of an oak
Then stops to show its prowess by bulging its throat
A clearing appears with its inviting center
It is a place to stay and absorb free solace —
A place of wished for peace along with craved tranquility

A choice of remaining

A choice for living

Oneness in the open arms of the meaning of life.

Acceptances

Where did we lose the days of waking up excited
About the future hours to come? How did fear
And anxiety creep into the marrow of our bones?
Maybe because we saw death take away so many things
We thought could never end. Maybe too many people
Told us that dreams were impossible to achieve – convinced us
That we needed to grow up and join the rest of the herd.

I know I have been abandoned so many times
I have lost count. Trust I placed got trodden down
As nothing more than a troublesome weed. I listened
And believed when told by others I wasn't good enough –
Especially from those I thought really cared for me. I
Allowed my self-confidence to become non-existent.
I learned too late the truths I needed to know – the jealousies,
The envies, the selfish motivations others used against me –
How they projected the warpedness of their own insecurities
Onto my aspirations. If I became successful they feared the loss
Of control over me and dreaded I would not need them
    anymore.

When I look down at graves, I cannot picture those I loved in
> oblong

Boxes rotting in the dirt. They were so much more. Because

Of that, I cannot bring myself to go to the cemetery. The
> vibrancy of

Their memory in my mind far surpasses the need for sadness
> at their passing.

My love has no need for proximity to decaying remains.

I now have to live days by looking for what is positive in the fact

That I woke up. There is a searching for types of upliftment

That used to come naturally. I have to accept

That the days of excitedly looking forward have

Slipped away.

But these acceptances are so hard –

Oh, so hard!!

Nine Pines

Together we dug the holes

My foot to the shovel

Arm muscles to pull and pile dirt

Her hands lovingly massaging new soil

Saving displaced worms to put back

Mixing and turning over mixtures

Jugs of fresh water filling the holes

Then root balls into the void

Fertile earth added and tamped

Her delicate hands transferring love

Extra water to top the mound

We planted our nine pine trees

One after another

We touched each with affection

And well-wishes

Some were thin as a plastic straw

Some were three, four, five feet tall

We had dug them up from by the pond

Our sweat we gladly shed

But as time passed

Not all made the transfer

Sadness for their failed valiant efforts

Squeezed our well-meaning hearts
The growth of the hardy ones filled us
With joy
Green needles grew long
Trunks thickened with peeling bark
Breezes hissed through the needles
Shade began to be seen
Months and years passed
Taller and taller they became
New blooms of fascicles slowly emerged
These strong tall pines reminded us
Of the planting we had shared together.

Silence of the Night

Tears well in my eyes for the wonders I have missed

Hardships try to overwhelm all that is good

I hear the loud silence flowing in the night air

Waiting for the sound of myself to be found in my cries

I can find a sadness in the shortness of life

I can find elation in the victory over evil

I see my own ineptitude at bringing peace

I find my intolerance and judgmentalism repulsive

Some people cannot reach as far to grasp their dreams

Visions of possibilities are not always the same

I look into the deep black sky filled with stars

I am reminded of so many forgotten elements of my life

I let slip away my purity and innocence

I traded in lies and deceits of a world gone mad

I feel hollow with unfulfilled potential

I suffer deeply remembering the hurt I have brought to others

Trusts I carelessly crushed and betrayed

My tears fall for too many things I cannot fix

The tears fall for a shortened future where I

      Will not have enough time to do better

Awaken! Oh please awaken to the glory of my soul

Wipe away my helpless ignorance of mind

Let promising light of the blazing stars

Fill this empty hull as a universe of teeming glinting purpose.

Painter's Touch

Swipe the broadest brush across your canvas,
Let swirl the bright colors of imagination
See all you want to see with your glorious eyes
Let the good side of the world enliven your mind;

Fast running time blurs the softest of lines
Step out of the relentless stream to personal stillness
Block out continual demands whipping around you
Breathe in what you feel outside of yourself;

I have known the vulnerability beneath the skin,
Seen the havoc, destruction and confusion simmering,
But the beauty of belief rides high above them all,
Your spirit rises against the tide to a victory of salvation;

The canvas fills with awe-inspiring joyfulness
Others can learn from your mind's creation
It will live well beyond your lifetime dreams
Brushstrokes paint the way to tranquil release.

Not Forgotten

Katydids call on a warm humid night
> From heavy bark and leaves of lazy live oaks
>> We walk hand-in-hand to music in our minds
>> Remembering the many other times of love –

Long nights of needed affection through joining of lips,
> Of falling asleep, she with her head on my shoulder,
>> I would hear her soft breathing
>> Along with the soothing sound of a night bird close by –

But for tonight it is the walk of oneness memory,
> The sweetest scent of blossoming gardenias,
>> Moonlight in her magnificent eyes,
>>> The recognizable soft smile on her lips,
>> The unspoken gratitude for our shared comfort,
The need for Katydid song to our ears.

❧❧❧

You Were Warned

The train rocked side to side in ordinary fashion
A clear widow let me watch the landscape whisk by –
Trees and posts and wide green fields with cattle grazing
A sliding panorama versus my stagnant life;

The black soft leather book rested on my thigh
I covered it with my black hat and hoped
The contents would soak directly in
So that when I put the hat back on my head
I would know all that was contained inside.
Silly? Sure. But imagination can accomplish great things.
Every once in a while my brain takes a left instead of a right
Besides, it worked for the guy in seat 236 two cars in front of me;

A tall gentleman of high cheek bones sat down next to me
His pure white hair looked falsely perfect
"You're facing a time you did not foresee,
A time when you try to look past the stop sign
And find there is absolutely nothing there,
But you are demanding something out of nothing.
As incomprehensible as it sounds, it is equally true.
Get your balance. Prepare yourself.
It's a long road to nowhere."

Without fanfare or introduction
He left as quickly as he had appeared.

I forgot what the ticket said of where I was going
The train was slowing, a shade was down over the window
The car I was riding in was empty
I picked up my hat and placed it on my head –
          the book was gone from my leg –
As the train came to a stop and the doors hissed open,
I stepped off the train as it dissolved behind me
There was nothing in front, below or above me –
I could only feel my presence but not see my body
I was neither excited nor apprehensive – I was nothing.
"Welcome to the other side of the stop sign,
Now let's see how creative you are."

Counterclockwise

My mind withdraws

The world turns oddly white

Misty

Thought runs amuck

I see my demise

In a crucified series

Of confusion

Abandonment

Just God and I

Heading on a collision

Course

To where

I do not know

I hold my breath

Yet try to breathe

I pray for help

For this incomprehensible

Loss of function

Scrambled sensory input

Senseless fear

For what is happening to me

No one can tell

The horror in my mind
The alarms sounding
Loud on over-sensitized ears
Only thought of here and now
No tomorrow seems possible
Anxiety strewn footpaths
Throw more nothingness at me
Sleep tempts
But cannot be –
Only one word repeats
"Stop"
I want to get away
I want to know why
I have become
Nothing more than a raw nerve
Thrashing about
Like a worm on hot concrete
I want my face to return
My heart of love to feel
My sphere of sanity replenished
I want to believe
I am more than this exploded consciousness

I need a shroud
To be thrown over the chaos
An umbrella to shield me
From this storm
Pluck me from this tornado
I beg of you
Do not leave me here.

Could We?

If hands could be boxes, just think

of how much more they could hold. Cold

sheets in November are certainly no fun

at all but the warmth of you made everything

seem worthwhile after the night time breezes

had finished with us. In the silence of the darkness

I have noticed how noisy a living body can be – deep breathing,

whistling exhales, grunts or groans, errant involuntary sounds.

They are certainly the sounds of living a normal life.

Who would want to collect dead butterflies when the wonders of

their beauty lies in their flight and flitting and landing

on delicate leaves in the garden. This has always reminded

me of your propensity to live in the freedom of the moment –

a state in which I am dismally deficient. Could we run in the

fields again? Look in awe at blue mountain tops? Dream of

France in the vividness of Spring? All things we loved to do

so many years ago. Maybe another time. For now I am content

to watch you sleep in the covers of our love.

Talk is Cheap

They say talk is cheap
But only when the words are few and
Often repeated.
Maybe I should talk to her more,
but what good would that do?
Her ability to listen died with her mind.
She no longer speaks to me,
her gaze remains fixed on the wall.
When she could still talk, I remember her pointing
And saying "I know that's a chair but I don't know
what that means. It doesn't mean anything to me."
We, on the other hand, understood without understanding.
When you can see, how can you know what blindness is?

The sidewalks fill with people every day,
Do we care what they think or feel?
Absolutely not. We remain locked in our tiny worlds
Believing what is in our minds is the only thing of importance.
It would seem obvious then
When we lose the ability to think
It is actually of no consequence at all.

Peace and Plenty

The door opened and she stepped into beauty

A world holding out its hand to her fascinated mind

Woods surrounded the cabin on three sides

Fresh oxygenated air permeated the scene

Morning light invigorated like fine art depictions

In colors from a master's palette

And she let the hand of the world be her guide.

She turned and knelt at her flower bed of

Daisies and petunias and lilies

Pulled tiny sprouting weeds

Her fingers loosening some dark rich earth

Then tamped it back down with practiced gentleness

While she talked to the many singing birds

Red wing blackbirds, cardinals, black-capped chickadees,

Bluebirds, ravens, woodpeckers – she loved them all

She filled the hanging feeders with seed,

Hung suet on the trunk of an ancient tree,

Filled the hummingbird feeder with red nectar

Scattered crumbled bread for the larger birds

Inside once again she watched from the kitchen window

As many of the birds descended to eat

Squirrels gathered under the platter to grab cast off sunflower seed.

Her fascination continued till the crowd dwindled to zero.

Outside then she sat on the green whicker chair,

Bible in her lap and prayer on her lips

Satisfied birds called and sang from high in the trees

A baby red-tailed fox appeared

climbed eagerly onto the porch

"well good morning my pretty little thing"

She produced a small red apple from in her apron

The fox took it gingerly then raced off the porch

And disappeared to enjoy its daily treat.

The Bible fell open to the well-worn Psalm pages

She reverently recited and prayed

In the peace and plenty of her cabin home.

Contrasts

Solemn days of sadness arrive unbidden
With the slow rising of the morning sun
Other houses peopled with those of pain and anguish
Come alive too to face another day;

Damp grass and shriveled toad stools gather on the lawn
Doves and grackles forage for seed in tall weeds
Blue jays call fervently for mates while females
Squawk and swoop because of eggs in the nest;

Abnormal and normal rolling side-by-side
It's hard for either to pay attention to the other
Yet there they are locked in their own spheres of existence
Repetitive and isolated without really being alone.

Who is missing and who is gone rides in their minds
Emptiness of former sheets and silent former wings
There is a mourning sound in distinct bird calls
As quiet tears fall from sad eyes inside;

The glory of morning dampened by shared grief
Neither one capable of comforting the other
So many miles apart for direct communication
Yet so near in distresses of the heart.

A Time of Questions

Where has my life gone?
We all ask that question when it's time,
The softness of eastern dawns
The glory of western sunsets
Change to an unexpected commonality
That disappoint our wished for old excitements.
What my eyes have seen
Is beginning to fade away due to sincere
Lack of caring. What to do about the fade?
It sneaks up on you so you cannot duck,
It robs you so stealthily, it slides by unnoticed.
Locked doors and closed windows
Provide no defense. Selfish prayer provides humor.
It's like being in a boat without a rudder,
Turning pleasant streams into fearsome straits
Slamming and banging you hither and thither
Until dizziness and shock are all that remain.
I try to open my eyes to a new dawn
Where the old feeling of well-being resided
But today is no longer that day
Sadly
Neither will tomorrow be.

Who Will Be the One?

I climb the stairs for a higher destination

Truth always seems to drift above me

Reaching for it only gets your hand slapped

Others don't want you to know they have no idea what it is either.

"I want to live a long time" you say

Believing you can stay just the way you are

Old age infirmity only happens to weaker people

"That is never who I will be"

And you could very well be right – death can snatch you away

In an accident, an embolism, a heart attack, a bullet

And there definitely would be no possibility

Of an old age facility in your arrogant future.

When the time comes to lay myself down

I do not wish to wait in empty silence

Hearing only the high whistling in my ears

Clasping my own hands to check if I'm still here.

Will you read to me even if I doze off?

Will you touch and hold my hand like days of love?

Will you be the one who says "I am with you."

On the Quiet Side

On the quiet side of the blinds
I wonder what horror is playing
There are no new ones
Just retreads in clearer disguise
Disease is disease, murder is murder,
Death – it's all the same as the centuries
Why do we keep expecting
Something different from ourselves?

Disaster follows us like a lost puppy
An amused cat watches and licks its paw
Being saved is a trick of the mind
Graveyards are filled with true Believers

I walk among the hills of plenty
Life runs, skitters, flies at my passing
It is a momentary snapshot
Of simple truth in 'here and then gone'

I once thought of beauty, not danger
Nighttime as refreshing, not evil
Warnings were enough to keep us safe
Secrets were exciting, not twisted

Sure, being naïve was its own reward
So many things I would rather not know
For now I have to sit behind closed blinds
To avoid becoming one of them.

Private Imagination

The sky had turned to an umbrella of gray
Birds flew back home to quietly wait for the sun

I followed the gravel strewn walkway
Tall bamboo framed me on either side

A large turtle ambled its way across the path
Waddling side to side, stopping only long enough

To make sure I was no threat before continuing
On its way to the refreshing waters of the pond.

Soft whisperings of thin pointy bamboo leaves
Caressed my ears in the kind breezes accompanying

My every step as if I was in another time and place
On my way to an excitingly mysterious destination.

My mind filled with flashes of waterfalls and tall trees
Swift flowing crystalline streams of cold refreshment

Deer running happily through protective woods
Ducks flying in v-formation behind their honking leader

I could breathe in deeply of the wonderfully clean air
I reached the hill at the end of the walkway and climbed up

Looked across the meadows and pastures till I spotted the horses
I wished I could be riding one, galloping in the wind,

Free to be ourselves united in our glorious freedom
Feeling the creak of leather and tinkling of metal rings

Travelling to our own secret places at thrilling speed
Where we could stop and stare in awe at creation.

With a smile on my face, I turned back to follow my walkway –
My private dreamland of exhilarating imagination.

c*⁀ഗഩ⁀ↄ

Her Time of Down and Up

She sat atop the levee

Her mind remembering

And trying not to remember

At the same time

Early evening sun setting

No beauty or fanfare attendant

Just an impotent coppery ball

Disappearing behind clouds

Where had those she loved gone?

Mothers, fathers, sisters, grannies?

Even pets of dogs, cats, hamsters.

All gone away to the unseen place.

A riverboat horn blared

Her eyes scanned the river waters

Till she spotted the tug

It reminded her of times of reading

About paddle-wheeled gambling boats

Meandering up and down the Mississippi

Carrying liquor, gambling, those carousing

Behind clouds of cigar smoke

And laughter and more drinks

The boats could take her away

From her loneliness and aloneness

Her sadness and despair

The antidote to depression

Fun without purpose

Wastefulness without regret

Chance adventure without fear

Up on deck

Watching the huge paddle blades

Churn up the foaming river waters

While she listened to

The piano and banjos from down below

With dancers celebrating living

And the cooling breezes setting her free

She looked up

At the evening sky

Bright with stars

And clear moonlight

Remembering great romance

And deep love

Having been spread

Like an expansive manicured lawn

Across her life

The iron grip

Of malaise relaxed in her heart

Her lips moved to a practiced smile

A long satisfying breath

Rose across her chest

As she continued to watch

The slow lapping

Of the river's mighty strength.

The Road

Then they turned a corner and tried to say
it never happened because no right angles exist
in a circle (though I had no idea we were following
a circular path to nowhere). They sang
their bawdy songs in which I found no interest.
It was in an oath I had given to follow a straight
and narrow way far from the one traversed
by fallen angels within the band of Lucifer.
I was required to stop and look at my surroundings
to find that others had no idea how to remove
themselves from the wrong road simply due
to the fact they could not comprehend
that their choice had been defective from the start.

I began to run, in fear, to search for the stretch of road
that led to the narrow gate I was promised for
a life everlasting.

What if I didn't get there in time? Others called after me,
wondering why I had broken away to leave them
on their own. Still, I kept running, further and further away
from the familiar crowd.

I was in a wilderness where things threatened in the night
but I carried on as if I were sacrificing and fasting,
certain that angels were my unseen protection.
In deep prayer I called on His holy name constantly
in my wanderings. For how long I diligently searched
I do not know. When weariness tried to overcome me,
I prayed even louder and harder. I refused to give in
to physical weakness. I would rest when I was instructed
to do so. I well knew sacrifice instead of ease was required
to enter into the longed for Kingdom.

Finally, in the hazy distance, I heard them singing songs
of the New Israel with blessings heaped upon the people
of Zion for their obedience and faith in God. I ran
with even greater speed with my heightened sense of fervor
and joy at having been guided to be where I needed to be
by a single voice I recognized calling my name
in the sweetest sound that had ever struck my ears.

I fell in among the pious. Instinctively I knew the hymns
being sung and chanted, sending our joyful noise up
to the Lord. How much further we were to travel I

did not know, nor did I care. I knew where this road
would end and that would be more than good enough
for me.

Woah! Surprise!

Their eyes stayed fixed on me

As they swam straight toward me

I stood by the lake bank

Young alligators of three feet long

Nearby must have been a den

In overgrown aquatic cover at the shore

They jockeyed for position with small splashes

Then settled down to stare

Their bone armored backs shone wetly

A striped tail emerged every once in a while

I had only wished for a calming view

Of the lake in early summer

I had brought no meat they craved

There was no aggression

One emerged from the water

Strolled nonchalantly past me

And disappeared into the woods

For better hunting I supposed

I remained wide-eyed

Frozen in place

Heart pounding from adrenaline

As the others realized I was no threat
To them or their home
They began swimming and chasing
Each other
Suddenly from out of bushes
Twenty feet to the right
Came a huge splash and thrash
The water churned
Two large eyes
Rows of sharp hollow teeth
Turned toward me
A furry mammal body
Hung limply in her mouth
'Mom' I supposed it must be
We stared at each other
Wary but non-threatening
Respectful
She pulled herself
Higher in the water
Exposing her light colored chest
Shook her head violently
The prey secured in her snout

Causing her catch to come apart

Pieces flew into the lake

The young alligators scarfed up

The splashing pieces

As Mom swallowed the main body

Lake water returned to its calmness

All eyes again fixed on me

Nether curious enough about meaning

Nor brave enough to stay longer

I slowly backed away

Headed beck down the dirt road

To my pick-up

I smiled

Satisfied with having witnessed

Thrilling family life

(Maybe a bit too thrilling)

Of such awe-inspiring

Reptiles

Though I may have accidentally

Made food for nightmares

For many years to come

A Repeated Place

Wind and breezes taken for granted

Like the ideas of love and sleep

When I awoke to the brightness of morning

I craved feeling good by a source of moving water

I walked to the pond with my towel

Sat on the deep luxurious grass

Still damp from morning dew

I watched the inviting surface

Glimmering disturbances of fish snatching insects

The breeze wandered across the surface in ripples

Pine trees whispered their songs of love

My mind refreshed and invigorated

Felt as if the scene was playing just for me.

A six by four inch box turtle lumbered down the bank

Unceremoniously slid into the water

With just his head breaking the surface

While he scanned for the minnows he had disturbed

Distant birds sang their good-morning tunes

In every imaginable key

Through the fine morning air

I felt slow breeze over my exposed skin

And sighed at the simple wonder

Time passed in a slow flow like day dreaming
Taking me to these memorable private spaces
Until bright clouds
Began to gray over
Birds sang less at their approach
Frogs awoke and began mating calls
They too could smell the approach of rain
That unmistakable exciting aroma like no other
I reluctantly arose
Imagining my lost friends waving from the other bank
I missed them too
And headed back to the house
As the refreshing rain began to fall.

I See Nothing

Cover my head with a blanket of knowledge
Bring understandings to my deepest core

Let the world I see make sense to me
Grip me with meanings I can't ignore

The years tick by (we've heard this before)
Everything feels worse than when I was born

Overused words like *peace* or *love*
Only hold meaning at rallies and marches

Humanity is becoming smarter and more animalistic
Those two elements together can not be compatible

Science and philosophy have severely diverged
Creating a cesspool of foul obnoxious thought

Lakes of unsympathetic caring drown the few who do
The knowers of creation dwindle in number

Warning sirens of sure collapse are sounding
Many only plug their ears instead of reacting

Advances in ignorance are sprouting wings
Running behavior of the senses into the ground

Shall we all dig tunnels out of our graves?

Will there be outpourings of true justice and righteousness?

How many thousands of years must be repeated?

How many lives must be lived without learning reality?

I wish I could help with compassionate understanding

But my own blindness is in my way

A sight of a positive future reversal of now

Resides in a place too far away for me to see.

Marsha's Well

You and I shall dance away
the beautiful hours before us
smiling for our grand twirlings.

Your sparkling eyes fixed on mine
turn the world into emerald bliss
moving with us to softest rapture.

Here we are at the well of your being
invited to draw from its mysterious depths
to satiate a culmination of superb oneness.

Dance in celebration around this well
hands held together in forever mode
two hearts melding into one strong beat.

It is a time of jubilation for our souls
as two wandering human beings
fortunate enough to have found each other.

So let us dance to discovered memories
think of nothing more than pure emotion
dancing here at Marsha's marvelous well.

No Place for Nostalgia

Catastrophe lends its ear to the sane

Boxcars filled with mystery slide by

Overcast days attest to hidden affairs of the sun

Claustrophobic eyes dart to and fro

We insist on carrying out conspiracies

Aimed at helpless entities of faceless vulnerability

Who has hidden empathetic concern under a rock?

Buildings have faces and names no one remembers

Classic businesses disappear beneath new sheet rock

We can dig through the layers to find the past

Old doors with a dentist's name painted on glass

The drug store became a condominium

The suite of doctor's offices has become a gym

Retread, recycle, revitalize, renew

Discard it, conceal it, forget it,

The people and places of old have no meaning any more

We the living are the only ones who count

New money needs to be made, nostalgia being worthless

We need to forget that nothing lasts forever

Reminders of mortality have to be buried

What was once mighty has been made insignificant

Momma checked out and is not coming back.

Two Strokes of Midnight

1

Language irrelevant when a scream is heard

In the distance we cannot discern

Was it a child or an adult?

We listen more to validate what was heard

We stop and wait in our own silence

The scream – it sounds again

Should we respond? Should we help?

Is it real? Where is it coming from?

Nature wants us to run toward the sound

Instinct wants us to stay away

We wait more, hoping we won't have to decide

No more screams fly through the night air

We quickly lose thought of it

Curiosity drops and we move on.

2

Dogs start barking

Then the howling comes

Coyotes join in

Who is encouraging whom

Something in the howl of coyotes

Reminds us of death

Something in the howling of dogs
Reminds us of pain and fear
A full moon blasts its insanity
Something inside of ourselves
Just wants it to stop.

Leona & Ned

It could have been any day of the week

But it was a sunny Friday they chose

For their serene stroll through the botanical garden

Black-eyed Susan blooms on their tall green stalks

Gave sustenance to orange-winged butterflies

While dense bottlebrush bushes provided haven for bright
yellow-winged ones

Their eyes drank in the living sights like thirsty travelers

And, in fact, Leona and Ned were simply sightseers

Within this realm of greenery and flowers being protected

From the wrath of the world outside

Manmade water features provided scenes of turtles swimming

And climbing up onto shady islands of brush and popcorn trees

Leona and Ned sat on wooden benches breathing in the
freshness

As they held hands in the peacefulness that surrounded their
special day

It was their fifth anniversary of having met in a setting just like this

An anniversary they never missed to celebrate in this manner

Honey bees buzzed on their way to the blooming clover

Geese climbed into the water in search of satisfying fish

Orange day lilies budded and blossomed along the pathway

An old thick oak tree was surrounded by ornamental boxwood
Like a green fluffy poodle hugging the legs of its master
Leona and Ned walked and kissed beneath the long arbor
Of Jacaranda trees in their fullness of majestic purple flowers
It was a Friday of good memories and satisfactions
A Friday of thankfulness among the designs of nature
A Friday of butterflies, blossoms, fragrances and
Love

Come Dance With Us

Soon they said we could come on out
Like ballet dancers to twirl about in
Delicate pirouettes to rhythmic notes
Of heart enlivening love for our ears;

Where we were had no meaning to us,
Simply the joy of such freedom of expression
Pushed us to wide grins and smiles
Cool air brushed past our spinning faces;

Here is where the world turned correctly
We reached for each other's hands
Formed our slow churning cone of unity
Spreading exuberance to every open corner;

Take us home together in our glee
To where we know cherished memory
Of dancing the celebrations of happiness
In never-ending smooth vibrations of ourselves.

Another Day

So many days I would go to the wharf,

Stroll down the rough spaced boards

Spaces showing like teeth for the orthodontist

Smell the water lapping at the pilings

Singing clapping songs about the sea

I lean on a railing of rough hewn wood

While avidly watching for acrobatic silver fins

Leap, fly, and dive into the water again.

I would imagine sailing on the glistening tide

To shores calling from distant horizons

I would smile in the shifting breeze,

Like a welcome face coming out of the weather

We should sail to nowhere in particular

Just so long as we wind up far away

In friendly waters of enticing invitation

Where only the sound of metal pulleys

Tinging on the mast measures our destiny

And gentle waves like beckoning fingerss

Lap scrumptiously against the fiber glass hull:

There would be night times watching skies

Zillions of stars like glitter scattered on black velvet

Inviting us to keep watching the majesty

Of all the mysterious distant suns

Creating moving fascination in our questing minds

Let us have the rocking of the boat

To imperceptibly close my eyes

For lulling me to deepest sleep.

'One day, one day that will be me'

Is what I told myself

The imaginary journey played strong

Then one day turned into another and another

Through sessions of life, living and misery,

The sailboat faded and faded some more

Until it disappeared altogether into a fog of

Where I could never find it again.

The wharf long since had been torn away

By relentless winds and waves of a hurricane,

But the aroma would still come to play in my head

To the memories of the shiny silver jumping fish

And sleeping under the ocean of stars.

No More Can I Run

I heard death come sniffing at the door
Before it jumped into bed with me.
Straightforward craftiness
It brought chills to prove its coldness
Far away I would rather be
In guaranteed places filled with promise
Unexpected ways creep across my being
A tightness gripping a lifeline rope
Death wants to squeeze its own agenda
Perhaps it wiil relinquish its hold
Perhaps a reprieve could be in order
Escape is a hopeful word
If I sleep
Will I wake?
It seems I am
Waiting for the judgment.

Fade to Sanity

In a room

Alone with my mind

I wonder what time it is

Not what the clock may indicate

But what time of life is this really

Which reality is this?

Younger ones sit up and don't care

Others shrug it off

Still others don't understand the question

For now I am chaotic

Tortured down to my deepest soul

I see walls that don't matter

Remember pasts that baffle me

Recall senseless interests

Conjure up faces from too long ago

If I don't care about what their names were

Why would anyone else find such thoughts valid

So, what time is it?

Recollections are useless here and now

Nostalgic memories are like stale bread

The room is dark

Just as my mind is shutting out the light

The smaller world

Is in the black shapes floating in the air

How they become even darker than darkness

Is worrisome – beyond my comprehension

You may shake your head

And say

"He must have lost his mind"

Still

The little boy sits in the dark room

Not knowing who he is.

www.ingramcontent.com/pod-product-compliance
Lightning Source LLC
Chambersburg PA
CBHW061400160726

47995CB00001B/393